- varying the sound level, from a whisper to a shout
- emphasising parts of the poem.

3 Practise reading together the parts for more than one voice.

## Talking about the poems

If you want to explore a poem through discussion it might help you to think of questions along these lines:

- What is the poem trying to say?
- How do I feel about the poem?
- What do I particularly like about the poem?
- Has the poem any special meaning for me?
- Are there any parts of the poem not clear to me?
- What do I think about the way it has been written (for example, whether it rhymes or not, its rhythm, its layout, its length, the way it sounds, whether lines and choruses have been repeated, and so on)?

## Performing the poems

Because the poems have speaking parts, they are rather like mini-plays which can be performed to an audience. If your group would like to perform some of the poems, you will find some detailed suggestions about how to do this at the back of the book.

# The mirror interview

**For two voices**

This is no ordinary interview. I have imagined a boy interviewing himself in a mirror just before his tenth birthday. (Have you ever done that?)

*Who are you?*

I'm trouble when my tongue
runs away with my sense.
I'm lazy when it's hot.
I fidget when I'm tense.

*Any daydreams?*

I get tunes in my ear
and pictures in my head.
I'm a conductor and an artist
when I dream in bed.

*Any problems?*

I'm clumsy with a ball
and hopeless with a pen.
But tomorrow is my birthday.
– I'm ten, ten, ten!

*Will that make a difference?*

I shall dazzle all my mates
with my great ideas
and make bullies tremble
with some scarifying fears.

*How come?*

I'll be double figures then
and that means double skills.
I'll be freer than an eagle
gliding over hills.

*What did you say you were?*

# Contents

# Introduction

## *Poems for more than one voice*

When you were very young I'm sure many of you enjoyed saying rhymes together with your parents and at school. Perhaps you still do.

But I expect that most of the poems you enjoy now were written for only one voice. When reading them aloud, you can share them but they were not written with that in mind.

The poems in this book and its companion volume have been written especially for sharing in a pair or group. They are poems with more than one voice, inviting you to take part in a group reading or perhaps a group performance.

They are poems to be read aloud and heard – just like the rhymes you joined in with when you were much younger. I hope you enjoy them.

## *Enjoying the poems*

There are three basic ways of enjoying these poems in a group.

### Reading aloud
1 Spend time in a group getting to know the poem by:
   • reading it to yourself
   • reading parts aloud together
   • trying different parts to see which combination of voices sounds best
   • sharing your first thoughts about the poem.
2 Decide together how each part should sound. Think about:
   • varying the speed of the reading
   • using pauses

220776

# The Midnight Party

## Poems for more than one voice

*Richard Brown*

CAMBRIDGE
UNIVERSITY PRESS

## Cambridge Reading

*General Editors*
Richard Brown and Kate Ruttle

*Consultant Editor*
Jean Glasberg

PUBLISHED BY THE PRESS SYNDICATE OF THE UNIVERSITY OF CAMBRIDGE
The Pitt Building, Trumpington Street, Cambridge CB2 1RP, United Kingdom

CAMBRIDGE UNIVERSITY PRESS
The Edinburgh Building, Cambridge CB2 2RU, United Kingdom
40 West 20th Street, New York, NY 10011-4211, USA
10 Stamford Road, Oakleigh, Melbourne 3166, Australia

First published 1993
Reprinted 1998 (twice)

Printed in the United Kingdom at the University Press, Cambridge

Typeset in Stone Serif

*A catalogue record for this book is available from the British Library*

ISBN 0 521 44587 6   paperback

I'm trouble with my tongue
and a dreamer too ...
but why ask all these questions?
Who are you?

*I'm trouble when my tongue
runs away with my sense.
I'm lazy when it's hot.
I fidget when I'm tense ...*

# What's in a name?

**For one voice and chorus**

Those of you who have a younger brother or sister, think back to the very first time you saw him or her. Can you remember the first time you used the baby's name? Was it anything like this poem?

When my new baby sister
first came home
I didn't want to look at her,
not at first.

Then I peeped
and I saw a tiny red face,
eyes closed
and little hands
that seemed lost.

*Sarah, Sarah, Sarah …*

She was so small.
Mum lifted her
onto the table.
How she cried.
She made me want to cry too.

*Sarah, Sarah, Sarah …*

I touched her
and called her name
for the first time:

*Sarah, Sarah, Sarah …*

Over and over I called her name
until it seemed to fit:

*Sarah, Sarah, Sarah …*

Then she turned her head
to look at me.
She was very quiet.
I whispered hello.

She held my finger
as if she never wanted
to let go.

*Sarah, Sarah, Sarah …*

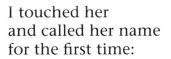

# Which name?

**For four voices**

I once knew a nine-year-old girl who was not entirely happy with her name. She asked me if I could think of a name which would suit her better. Nothing came to me at first, but after about ten minutes the name Lucy popped into my head. I knew this was the right name; it seemed to fit the girl like a glove. When I told her this she looked surprised. "But that's just what my dad says," she told me. A coincidence? I've used the memory of this in the following poem.

1 My name is Jo.

2   "Hi, Jo."

3   "How are you, Jo?"

1 That's what they call me.

4 *But I hear another name*
*whispered inside me:*
*Lucy, Lucy, Lucy.*

1 Mum chose Jo.
It's short for Josephine.

2   "Hi, Jo."

3   "How's school, Jo?"

1 That's what they call me.

4 *But I hear another name*
*whispered inside me:*
*Lucy, Lucy, Lucy.*

1 My middle name's Anastasia.
Dad chose it.
I never use it.
That's what they call me.

4 *But I hear another name*
*whispered inside me:*
*Lucy, Lucy, Lucy.*

1    If we could choose
the names we like
mine would be Lucy.
I'm Lucy inside.

4    *I hear that name
whispered inside me:
Lucy, Lucy, Lucy.*

1    Am I Lucy or Josephine?
Am I both or one?
If I am one, the other's a stranger.
How can I be a stranger to myself?

4    *I hear that name
whispered inside me:
Lucy, Lucy, Lucy.*

# Just don't call us names

**For four voices**

Name-calling is a nasty business whenever it happens. In this poem I have imagined a boy called James who has got into the habit of calling his brothers and sisters unpleasant names. They decide to put a stop to it.

**Younger brother**
You may be a shadow-boxer
or an all-in wrestler;
you may point your biggest finger
and jab it in the air.

**Younger sister**
You may scowl an ugly face-ache
and scream until you're ginger;
you may grin so slick and sly
and be terribly unfair.

**Older brother**
You may do all these things and more
my dear dear brother James,
but this I tell you loud and clear,
this I tell you brother dear:

**All**
JUST DON'T CALL US NAMES.
DO YOU HEAR? JUST
DON'T CALL US NAMES.

**Older sister**
You may think you're yodelling Tarzan
as you flex your puny muscles;
you may leap upon the settee
and swing towards the west.

**Younger brother**
You may wrestle with a tiger
and pretend to be a yeti;
you may lumber like an ape
and beat upon your chest.

12

**Older brother**
You may do all these things and more
my dear dear brother James,
but this I tell you loud and clear,
this I tell you brother dear:

**All**
JUST DON'T CALL US NAMES.
DO YOU HEAR? JUST
DON'T CALL US NAMES.

**Younger sister**
You may puff up like a pink balloon
and make rude popping noises;
you may wriggle all your fingers
in that stupid kind of way.

**Older sister**
You may flap your arms like dragons' wings
and blast the room to cinders;
you may bellow like an elephant
to keep us all at bay.

**Older brother**
You may do all these things and more
my dear dear brother James,
but this I tell you loud and clear,
this I tell you brother dear:

**All**
JUST DON'T CALL US NAMES.
DO YOU HEAR? JUST
DON'T CALL US NAMES.

**Older sister**
You may turn all soft and silly,
don't think I'm fooled by that;
you may say you're very sorry,
it's just a feeble act;
you may think I'm very stupid,
I'll never swallow that.

**Younger sister**
So remember what I tell you, James,
remember loud and clear:

**All**
JUST DON'T CALL US NAMES.
DO YOU HEAR? JUST
DON'T CALL US NAMES.

# Our street

**For five voices**

Where we live affects the way we feel about ourselves. In this
poem not everything is happy but it seems a friendly place.
How does it compare with where you live?

**All**  *In our street*
**1**  there are friendly houses
where we can stand on the step
and say hello.

**All**  *In our street*
**2**  there are sad houses
where the paint peels
and the curtains are closed.

**All**  *In our street*
**3**  there are warm houses
which call us in as if
we're part of the family.

**All**  *In our street*
**4**  there are scary houses
where people shout
and the weeds grow high.

**5**  At the end of our street
lives our Gran.
Snug as a tea-cosy,
she calls us her cup of tea.

# My tree

**A poem for reading around. The whole group should read the first four words of each verse.**

Have you ever planted a tree, bush or flower and watched it grow over a long period of time? If you have, you will know how special the plant can become to you – like the tree in this poem.

1   *When I was one* a little tree
    no bigger than a flower
    was planted in our garden.

2   *When I was two* it sent out
    bright little green hands
    that tickled me.

3   *When I was three* it was taller than me
    and a bird picked
    its three bright red berries.

4   *When I was four* I picked a leaf
    and chewed it. Horrible.
    I didn't like my tree that year.

5   *When I was five* I saw on a leaf
    a beautiful blue butterfly
    like a new flower.

6   *When I was six* my dad said
    the tree would have to be moved.
    I wouldn't let him: it had been there all my life.

7   *When I was seven* I tried to swing
    on its lowest little branch
    and it snapped. How sorry I felt.

8   *Now that I'm eight* I shelter under it
    and wait for a bird to build its nest there.

# Sometimes my sister

**For two voices**

Have you been teased by a brother, sister or friend? If you have, you will know why the same puzzled thought goes round and round inside the head of the child in this poem.

Sometimes my sister's not nice to me.
She combs my hair so hard it hurts.

*And yet Mum says my sister loves me.*

Sometimes my sister hides my things
and scribbles in my books. It hurts.

*And yet Mum says my sister loves me.*

Sometimes my sister pinches me
and whispers nasty things. It hurts.

*And yet Mum says my sister loves me.*

And at such times my sister and I
fight and cry. It hurts.

*And yet Mum says my sister loves me.*

Sometimes my sister can be nice.
Oh, yes, she can be nice.
She hugs me when I'm hurt
and holds my hand in the dark.
Oh, yes, Mum's right, she can be nice.

*Perhaps … my sister loves me.*

# Unhappy boy

**For one voice and chorus**

This is a poem about a boy who is becoming a playground bully.
I have often wondered why some children become bullies.
Perhaps there is a clue to the problem in the title of this poem.

He was standing in the playground
with his hands on his hips,
a scowl on his face
and a snarl in his lips.

*Feet well apart*
*and hair flying wild,*
*now who's going to dare*
*play with this child?*

He was roaring round the playground
a-fidget for a fight.
All turned away from him,
scared at the sight.

*Feet well apart*
*and hair flying wild,*
*now who's going to dare*
*play with this child?*

He was standing by the fountain
juggling with a stone.
The space around him grew and grew.
He knew he was alone.

*Feet well apart*
*and hair flying wild,*
*now who's going to dare*
*play with this child?*

# A playground chant

**For three voices and chorus**

I wonder how many playground chants you know?
Here is a new one to add to your collection.

1   See me here,
see me there,
think of me, I'm everywhere.
Be a sport,
be a friend,
never leave me till my end.

   *Tell a joke,
tell a fib,
poke a bully
in the rib.*

2   See me here,
see me there,
promise you will always share.
In a crowd,
all alone,
never feel you're on your own.

   *Step on lines,
kiss and chase,
hold your breath,
win the race.*

3   See me here,
see me there,
we can always be a pair.
Secrets too,
laughter long ...
sing again this playground song.

# Sporting wishes

**For six voices**

Do you have a favourite sport? And do you dream
sometimes of growing up to be a star in that sport?

1   I wish I was a champion swimmer
    streaking through the pool,
    faster, smoother, stronger
    than anyone at school.

**All** *Swish, splash,*
*swish, splash,*
*somersault the air;*
*breaststroke,*
*butterfly,*
*nothing can compare.*

2   And I a great cricketer,
    watch me smash a four,
    see the ball rise clean for six –
    a mesmerising score.

**All** *Swipe, cut,*
*swipe, cut,*
*slicing through the air;*
*runs come*
*thick and fast,*
*ready to declare.*

3   I wish I was a sprinter
    sizzling round the track,
    leaving the others far behind
    and never looking back.

**All** *Run, run,*
*streak ahead,*
*a bird upon the air;*
*breaking*
*every record,*
*yes, we know it's not fair.*

4  And I a world footballer
   shooting from midfield,
   such lightning passes, cunning feints,
   the others have to yield.

All  *Pass, run,*
     *trap, kick,*
     *headers in the air;*
     *goals to make*
     *the other team*
     *cry out in despair.*

5  I wish I was a tennis ace,
   the idol of the crowd;
   tense, exciting rallies and
   serves to make you proud.

All  *Love, fifteen,*
     *forty, deuce,*
     *cracking through the air;*
     *smash and lob*
     *down the line,*
     *extraordinary flair!*

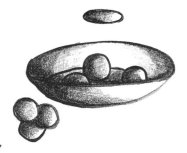

6  And me? Well –
   I'll stay a tiddlywinker,
   flicking counters back and forth,
   just playing with my aunty
   when I visit her up north.

All        *Tiddlywinker?*
(except     *Tiddlywinker?*
Speaker 6)  *That's all you want to be?*
           *Not televised*
           *and idolised,*
           *not famous, then?*
           *I see.*
           *Say no more about it, then,*
           *and do excuse me!*

# The pink party

**For two or more voices**

Have you ever been to a party with a colour theme?
Was it anything like this one?

1   Next Tuesday morning
        – we hope you will come –
    we're holding a party;
        it's sure to be fun.

2   It's going to be different
        – now please don't blink –
    it's a party where everything's
        going to be PINK.

1   Now wear pink shorts
        or a nice pink dress,
    and pink your hair –
        yes, nothing less.

2   Wear a pink top hat
        with a long pink scarf,
    some nice pink plimsolls
        – now please don't laugh.

All   *There'll be*
    *jellies and prawns and pink mayonnaise,*
    *strawberry tarts with a clear pink glaze,*
    *spam rolled up and ham served flat,*
    *a birthday cake like a big pink hat,*
    *pink champagne and little pink spoons,*
    *tiny pink biscuits shaped like moons.*

1   At the big pink door
        you must say hello,
    give a nice pink present,
        with a big pink bow.

**2**  You must wipe your feet
      on the pink doormat,
inflate a balloon
      like a big pink cat.

**1**  Run through the garden,
      join in the games,
come to the table
      and sit by your names.

**All**  *There'll be*
*jellies and prawns and pink mayonnaise,*
*strawberry tarts with a clear pink glaze,*
*spam rolled up and ham served flat,*
*a birthday cake like a big pink hat,*
*pink champagne and little pink spoons,*
*tiny pink biscuits shaped like moons.*

**1**  Next Tuesday morning
      – we hope you'll come –
it'll be the best party
      with the pinkest fun.

**2**  Yes, it's going to be different
      – and now you can blink –
the best party ever,
      everything PINK.

# The midnight party

**A poem for reading around**

Just imagine what it would be like if the woodland animals decided to hold a party. What would happen if an uninvited guest turned up … someone they all feared?

The Narrator's part is in italics (*like this*). You will need to watch out for it in the other parts as well.

**Owl**  Who will come to my midnight party?

**Narrator**  *said the owl to the rustling wood.*

**Cat**  I, *said the cat*, I'd certainly like that.
I will come to your party.

**Vole**  I, *said the vole*, though the night be black as coal.
I'll come to your party.

**Owl**  Who will bring food to my midnight party?

**Narrator**  *said the owl to the rustling wood.*

**Badger**  I, *said the badger*, I'm not a cadger.
I'll bring food to your party.

**Stoat**  I, *said the stoat*, I'll bring fish from the moat.
I'll bring fish to your party.

**Owl**  Who'll bring games to my midnight party?

**Narrator**  *said the owl to the rustling wood.*

**Mouse**  I, *said the mouse*, I've plenty in my house.
I'll bring games to your party.

**Mole**  I, *said the mole*, with my game of bowls.
I'll bring bowls to your party.

**Owl**  Who will dress up for my midnight party?

**Narrator**  *said the owl to the rustling wood.*

**Fox**  I, *said the fox*, with my bright red socks.
I'll dress up for your party

**Bat**  I, *said the bat*, with my two-pointed hat,
I'll dress up for your party.

| Owl | Who'll bring joy to my midnight party? |
|---|---|
| Narrator | *said the owl to the rustling wood.* |
| Moon | I, *said the moon*, with my silver spoon.<br>I'll bring joy to your party. |
| Narrator | *But then came a shriek in the rustling wood*<br>*and in the shadows an old witch stood.* |
| Witch | I, *said the witch*, with my terrible itch.<br>I'll bring joy to your party. |
| All | The owl flapped its wings.<br>The cat stole away.<br>The vole hid deep.<br>The badger wouldn't stay.<br>The stoat crept off.<br>The mole dug deep.<br>The bat flew aloft.<br>The moon fell asleep.<br>The fox padded free<br>and the mouse cried, "Flee!" |
| Narrator | *Then the owl turned its stare, its terrible glare,*<br>*on that witch a-twitch in the shadows.*<br>*And the old crone fled to her filthy bed.*<br>*Owl closed one eye.* |
| Owl | Tomorrow, *it said*, tomorrow for my midnight<br>party. |

# Mourning the moon

**For three voices**

In this poem I have tried to imagine how alarmed two baby owls
might be on first seeing the moon grow smaller and smaller.
They would be too young to know what was happening or
whether the moon would return. To them, the moon is a giant
friendly eye watching over them; so why is it slowly closing?

**Mother owl**
Two weeks you've been
afloat in this wood,
happy, exploring
the dark all you could.
So why do you stare
at the black of the sky
with strange looks of sadness
and soft hooting sigh?

**First baby owl**
When we first emerged
the night had an eye,
wide open, brilliant;
now it's closing – but why?

**Second baby owl**
It lit up each leaf,
the eye of a mouse,
made this old ruin
an enchanted house.

**Mother owl**
Too bright, perhaps,
but it helped you to see
where food and danger
lurked by the tree.

**First baby owl**
Now it's but a sliver,
a nibble of night,
the sky and this wood
consuming its light.

**Second baby owl**  The dark has closed
its big silver eye.
No gleam, no moonbeam:
you ask why we sigh?

**First baby owl**  Darkness is safe,
you've always said so,
but the moon was our first friend –
why did it go?

**Mother owl**  Do not fear, my babes,
the moon will return.
Of its moods you two
have much to learn.
Tomorrow, or soon,
there'll be a re-birth,
the moon will brighten,
re-silver earth.
So put away mourning,
no need to sigh,
the night will soon
re-open its eye.

# Down by the stream

**For three voices**

Those of you who go fishing or just enjoy sitting by a river will know the lazy mood this poem is trying to catch.

1  Down by the stream
2  down by the grass
3  down where the swans drift by
1  the wind is whispering in the reeds
All  *whisper*
  *whisper*
  *whisper*
  *whispering in the reeds.*

1  Down in the water
2  down in the weeds
3  down where the minnows speed
1  a frog is bubbling in the mud
All  *bubbling*
  *bubbling*
  *bubbling*
  *bubbling in the mud.*

| | |
|---|---|
| 1 | Up in the trees |
| 2 | up in the leaves |
| 3 | up where the crow sits hunched |
| 1 | a kite is flapping in the breeze |
| All | *flapping* |
| | *flapping* |
| | *flapping* |
| | *flapping in the breeze.* |
| 1 | Up in the sky |
| 2 | up in the grey |
| 3 | up where a plane drones by |
| 1 | the sun is breaking through the clouds |
| All | *breaking* |
| | *breaking* |
| | *breaking* |
| | *breaking through the clouds.* |
| 1 | Down on the bank |
| 2 | down on the grass |
| 3 | down where the river's blue |
| 1 | my head is writing this short poem |
| All | *writing* |
| | *writing* |
| | *writing* |
| | *writing …* |

# Winter's song

**For three or more voices**

This poem was written in November when winter was about to set in. It was triggered by the first two lines of a poem by Rachel Field called "Something told the wild geese", which begins,
"Something told the wild geese
it was time to go ... "
Those two lines stuck in my mind so much it seemed as if they insisted on being put into a new poem.

1  Something told the wild birds
it was time to fly,
time to gather in a flock
and wheel across the sky.

2  Out into the sunset,
over distant sea,
listening for the wind
in an African tree.

All  *Swish-swish our wings go,*
*swish-swish the breeze;*
*some of us won't make it*
*over endless seas.*

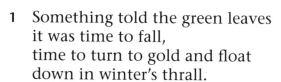

1  Something told the green leaves
it was time to fall,
time to turn to gold and float
down in winter's thrall.

2  Falling in the sunset
onto chilling grass,
turning in the frost as
brittle as glass.

All  *Swish-swish the wind goes,*
*swish-swish the breeze;*
*all of us are falling*
*in a sweep of leaves.*

30

1 Something told the wild things
 it was time to sleep,
 time to curl up in the dark,
 safe from winter deep.

2 Deep in every burrow,
 dark in hidden nest,
 slower, slower heartbeats
 in a dreamless rest.

All *Swish-swish the wind goes,*
 *swish-swish the breeze;*
 *over every burrow*
 *in the winter's freeze.*

1 But something told the robin
 it was time to be,
 time to sing a winter song
 in a silent, glittering tree.

2 Bobbing on the garden wall,
 hopping to and fro,
 an ember of a fireball
 in the diamond snow.

All *Swish-swish the wind goes,*
 *swish-swish the breeze;*
 *cold the song of winter*
 *through the whitened trees.*

# A winter chant

**For three voices and chorus**

This is just the sort of poem you could chant to yourself as you trudge through the snow, perhaps with your friends.

*Light fox footfalls,*
*hard white snow,*
*light frost-diamonds,*
*bare bright bush.*

1   Mouths are muffled,
shoes are scuffled.
feet go crunch, crunch, crunch.
Here lies rabbit trail,
here scrapes badger tail,
here the puddle goes crack, crack, crack.

*Light fox footfalls,*
*hard white snow,*
*light frost-diamonds,*
*bare bright bush.*

2   Songs are smothered,
coats are covered,
birds go flap, flap, flap.
Here lie pigeon feet,
here pecks robin's beak,
stones on the pond go clink, clink, clink.

*Light fox footfalls,*
*hard white snow,*
*light frost-diamonds,*
*bare bright bush.*

**3** Night is falling,
snow is thickening,
streetlight glitters on the ground;
snowmen dreaming,
windows steaming,
muffled moonlight, and no sound.

# Never, always

**A chant for two voices**

This is a fun poem to be chanted, perhaps while patting hands together. It contrasts the generous person with the mean, the optimist with the pessimist.

If I sing it
if I say it
if I write it in my book –

    *Never sing it*
    *never say it*
    *never write it in your book.*

If I taste it
if I touch it
if I give it, go on, look –

    *Never taste it*
    *never touch it*
    *never give it, I shan't look.*

If I lend it
if I keep it
if I leave it in the car –

    *Never lend it*
    *never keep it*
    *never leave it in your car.*

If I paint it
if I snap it
if I shout it to a star –

    *Never paint it*
    *never snap it*
    *never shout it to a star.*

I shall know it
I shall be it
I shall see it inside out.

*Never know it*
*never be it*
*never see it inside out.*

Why d'you say that?
What's the problem?
Tell me what it's all about.

    *Never sing it*
Always sing it
    *Never say it*
Always say it
    *Never write it*
Always write it
    *Never taste it*
Always taste it
    *Never touch it*
Always touch it
    *Never lend it*
Always lend it
    *Never pinch it*
As if I would!
    *Never paint it*
If I could!
    *Never snap it*
Why ever not?
    *Do you hear me?*
Never – what?

# Night street

**For three voices**

Ordinary noises heard in the daytime can sometimes sound strange and frightening at night. In this poem, three children half-asleep in their beds hear footsteps. Is it Dad coming home?

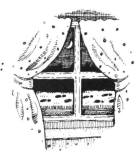

**All**  *Half-asleep and half-awake,*
*who can tell what's true?*
*Footsteps in the street outside:*
*Dad, can that be you?*

1  As I lay in my bed
with the moon on my sheet,
I heard the soft thud
of a giant's feet. Scared,

I quivered,
shook and
shivered,
huddled in the dark.
All at once –
a silence
and a lone dog's bark.

**All**  *Half-asleep and half-awake,*
*who can tell what's true?*
*Footsteps in the street outside:*
*Dad, can that be you?*

2  As I lay in my bed
clasping my sheet,
not a giant I heard,
but a dragon's feet. Scared,
I shivered,
terrified,
quivered,
huddled in my bed.
All at once –
a silence
pressing round my head.

**All**  *Half-asleep and half-awake,*
      *who can tell what's true?*
         *Footsteps in the street outside:*
         *Dad, can that be you?*

**3**  As I lay in my bed
    tight in my sheet,
    I heard nothing but the patter
    of goblin feet. Scared,

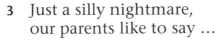

         I shivered,
         shook and
         gibbered,
         hiding in my bed.
         All at once –
         a laugh
         cackled in my head.

**All**  *Half-asleep and half-awake,*
      *who can tell what's true?*
         *Footsteps in the street outside:*
         *Dad, can that be you?*

**1**  At night our street's mysterious,
    full of ghostly sound …

**2**  Heavy footsteps, whisperings,
    make our hearts pound.

**3**  Just a silly nightmare,
    our parents like to say …

**All**  *Giant, dragon, goblin?*
      *Only light keeps them at bay.*

# Into the sea

**For one voice and chorus**

Not everything is friendly about the seaside, is it?

*So cold it is,*
*so rough the waves*
*down in the stirring water-caves.*

1  Give me your hand
we'll dash the hot sand
where beach balls bounce and splash.

Give me your hand,
we'll fly the hot sand
to the curving wave and crash.

*So cold it is,*
*so rough the waves*
*down in the stirring water-caves.*

1  The sand's so hot
we must dance and spin.
The noise of the waves
comes dashing in.

Give me your hand
and lead me there
into the waves
as deep as you dare.

*So cold it is,*
*so rough the waves*
*down in the stirring water-caves.*

# The Pied Piper's return

**For up to six voices**

The story of the Pied Piper of Hamelin was told in a long poem
by Robert Browning over a hundred years ago. The town of
Hamelin was overrun with rats. The Pied Piper charmed them a
away with his magic flute, but when the mayor refused to pay
him for this service, the piper charmed all the town's children
away too, in revenge. They disappeared inside a mountain, neve
to be seen again. Only one child, a lame boy, escaped to tell
the tale. In the poem that follows, I have tried to imagine what
would happen if the Pied Piper turned up at a school like yours

1   Two by two, two by two,
     a crocodile, we go,
out the school and past the shops,
     starting quiet and slow.

**All**   *A strange man is leading us,*
*a bell upon his head,*
*a jester in a jolly suit,*
*his face a glowing red.*

2   Two by two, two by two,
     a crocodile, we dance;
so much energy in our limbs
     we skip, we laugh, we prance.

**All**   *A strange man is leading us,*
*playing hard his flute.*
*Music, music everywhere*
*bewitching every boot.*

3   Two by two, two by two,
     a crocodile we stay;
   hand in hand into the woods,
     shadows dark and grey.

**All**   *A strange man is leading us*
*and we are growing tired.*
*The heavier grow our smarting feet*
*the faster he is fired.*

**Piper**   I play fast
upon my flute,
never more
shall I be mute.
Never more
shall I forgive ...
but I will let
these children live.
Never shall they
change, grow old;
a thousand years
and never cold.

4   Two by two, two by two,
     oh, will we ever stop?
We're scared now and aching;
     some of us will drop.

**All**   *A strange man is leading us*
*down into a cave.*
*We've barely strength enough ... must try*
*to turn our heads and wave.*

5   Two by two, two by one,
     alone because he's lame,
Thomas on the echoing road;
     he'll never be the same.
Two by two, two by one,
     we dance without a thought.
Poor Thomas sits upon the road,
     a wild thing caught.

**Piper**   I play fast
upon my flute,
never more
shall I be mute.
Never more
shall I forgive …
but I will let
these children live.
Never shall they
change, grow old;
a thousand years
and never cold.

**All**   *A strange man is leading us*
*into a world of dreams;*
*the mountain's other sunny side*
*where nothing's what it seems*

*where nothing's what it seems.*

# The spirit of place

**A poem for four voices**

Here is just the beginning of a horror story. Where will it end?

1   There was a sea
2   a blue sea
3   a secret blue sea
4   and in this sea
1   there was an island
2   a spiky island
3   a spiky green island
4   and in this island
1   there was a valley
2   a deep valley
3   a hot deep valley
4   and in this valley
1   there was a tree
2   a vast tree
3   a vast ancient tree
4   and in the roots of this tree
1   there was an egg
2   a historic egg
3   a prehistoric egg
4   and in this egg
1   there was a creature
2   a live creature
3   a creature so wild
4   so full of energy
All   *the old tree trembled.*

1   And in a hurricane
2   a tearing hurricane

| | |
|---|---|
| 3 | a fierce tearing hurricane |
| 4 | that tree cracked |
| All | *cracked to the roots.* |
| 1 | And out of those roots |
| 2 | those shattered roots |
| 3 | roots laid bare in the howl |
| 4 | climbed the creature |
| 1 | the wild creature |
| 2 | so full of energy |
| 3 | so full of destruction |
| 4 | it shrieked for escape. |
| 1 | There was a sea |
| 2 | a blue sea |
| 3 | a boiling blue sea |
| 4 | and in this sea |
| 1 | there was an island |
| 2 | a spiky island |
| 3 | an island in turmoil |
| 4 | and at the edge of this island |
| 1 | was the creature |
| 2 | the wild creature |
| 3 | the creature so full of destruction |
| 4 | it was ready to plunge |
| 1 | plunge into the sea |
| 2 | the boiling sea |
| 3 | and swim, swim, swim |
| All | *towards us all.* |

# The nursery ward

**For six voices**

In this hospital you will be surprised how many of the patients
you already know.

**Narrator**  All was quiet on the Nursery Ward.
The clock ticked loudly, the patients snored.
The nurse was humming, the doctor sang ...
until, that is, the telephone rang.

**Ambulance woman**  Is that you, Doctor? Ambulance here.
I'm bringing in twins, quite injured I fear.
One's Jill, her brother's called Jack.
Both their heads have a nasty crack.

**Doctor**  Now, quickly, Nurse, get them into bed.
I shall examine their battered heads.
Get some towels and fetch the vapour;
we'll need some vinegar and tough brown paper.

**Narrator**  Jack felt poorly, it made Jill wince;
her head felt like a pound of mince.

**Nurse**  Now don't make a fuss, just hold still,
or I'll give you both a sleeping pill.

| | |
|---|---|
| **Narrator** | Jack was shaking, and Jill was a-flutter, when in came a girl with a nervous stutter. Her shoulders shook and her eyes grew wider as she whispered a tale of a big black spider. |
| **Miss Muffet** | I was quietly supping my curds and whey, when down dropped the spider, as if to say, "With my hairy legs and my beady eye, I'd make a handsome friend. Oh, give it a try." |
| **Narrator** | But then Miss Muffet was drowned by a call: |
| **Doctor** | Nurse, quick, quick – he fell off a wall. Just a pile of pieces that look like shell … |
| **All** | It's Humpty Dumpty, far from well. |
| **Narrator** | Poor Humpty in fragments was laid on a bed. They found the bits that made his head. |
| **Doctor** | We shall stick him together, his arm, his leg … but I'm afraid he'll look like a crazy egg. |

**All**   Now Jack sat up
and Jill looked round,
Miss Muffet stared
without a sound.
They watched as Nurse
and Doctor too
made Humpty's head
look almost true.
"Hurrah," said Jack.
"Hurray," said Jill.
Miss Muffet smiled
and refused a pill.
And just as all
seemed rosy then
there came the clamour
of thousands of men.

**Ambulance woman**   Is that you, Doctor? Ambulance here.
I've got ten thousand soldiers blasting my ear.
The Duke of York's men are thronging the streets.
They say they've got blisters all over their feet.

**Doctor**   Blisters? How many? Twice ten thousand soles?
Nurse, start to prepare ten thousand foot-bowls.
We'll need millions of plasters, and mustard too.

**Narrator**   Nurse scurried away. Miss Muffet said, "Phew!"

Amidst all the racket there came a loud sneeze,
then a snuffle, a snishoo, a very bad wheeze.

**Dr Foster**  Oh, dear, what's wrong? I'm just back from
      Gloucester.
I'm soaking wet through. Yes, it's me, Doctor
      Foster.

I caught such a cold, I feel I could die –

**Narrator**  When from Humpty's bed came a terrible cry.
One of York's men had stepped on his shell,
and now he was feeling – well, dreadfully unwell.

**All**  And that's not all!
Then Jack fell down
(and Jill tried to paper
the crack in his crown).
Miss Muffet's eyes
grew that much wider
when into the ward
came the hairy spider.
Humpty lay groaning,
holding his head
as ten thousand soldiers
camped round his bed.
Coughing quite badly,
poor Doctor Foster
rang for a taxi
to take him to Gloucester.

**Doctor**  We've never been busier, have we, Nurse?
**Nurse**  Never, dear Doctor, I've not seen worse.

# Performing the poems

Reading a poem aloud is one thing. Acting it is quite another. When you act a poem you must know the words by heart and have prepared suitable actions, perhaps even sound effects, to go with them. Acting a poem is like putting on a mini-play for your audience.

If you would like to perform some of these poems, you may find the following advice useful. Discuss the points in your group and with your teacher. Specific suggestions for individual poems are on pages 50–56.

## General points

1 Who will be your audience? Have you chosen a poem you think they will like and understand?
2 Are you really interested in the poem yourself? Is it one you want to spend time on? Is it one you want to learn by heart and share with others?
3 Do you feel comfortable working with the people in your group?
4 Do you all understand the poem you have chosen? If not, talk about what puzzles you. You can often understand a poem better by sharing what you think about it with others.
5 Between you, choose the parts of the poem you are going to perform carefully. Is your voice the most suitable one for your part?
6 Together, read the poem aloud several times. Talk about how each part might sound. Ask yourselves these questions:
   • Are there parts which need to be faster or slower than others?
   • Do some parts need to be louder or quieter than others?

- Are there any parts or sounds which need emphasising?
- Would sound effects help?

7 Next, as a group, copy the poem into the middle of a large sheet of paper. Make notes around the poem to remind yourselves what was agreed. You can underline certain words or highlight them. This will be your working script.

8 Practise reading the poem into a tape recorder. Play it back and discuss how it might be improved.

9 Parts of some of the poems are spoken by two or more voices together. These are usually marked **All** which refers to all those who have parts in the poem. Sometimes, however, parts for more than one voice are printed in italics and this allows for other people, who may not have a part, to join in. This is usually called a chorus. Practise the chorus carefully so that everyone knows exactly how to say it and the words remain clear.

10 Now learn your part of the poem by heart. When you perform your poem you won't be *reading* it, you will be *performing* it. There is a big difference. Your performance will be more like something acted on the radio than read from a page.

11 Next, rehearse your "mini-play" together. Tape it again, and listen to how it sounds. Do you need to make any final changes? You could ask one or two friends what they think of it.

12 At this point you will need to decide whether any mime, movement or acting would help make the poem more enjoyable for the audience. If you do not want to do this yourself, another group might be willing to mime actions while you perform the poem.

13 Only perform your poem when you all feel confident. It will help the audience if one of

you introduces the poem, saying where it is set and what it is about.

This preparation is likely to take quite a time, especially if the poem is a long one. It can't always be done in one session. You may well not have enough class time for it, so think about getting together at lunchtime, after school or at weekends.

## *Suggestions for individual poems*

### The mirror interview
1 Face each other. Copy your partner's movements, as in a mirror image.
2 Some of the lines could have actions with them. For example, fan yourself when you say it's hot; conduct an orchestra; paint like an artist; drop a ball; look fierce when you make bullies tremble.
3 The voices change places at the end. What would it sound like if the poem was repeated with the parts exchanged? Try it.

### What's in a name?
The chorus which repeats the name Sarah should start with a faint whisper and gradually increase in volume until it sounds normal.

### Which name?
1 Voice 1 should sound thoughtful, even serious. Voices 2 and 3 should be bright and cheerful.
2 The name Lucy must be whispered. The fourth voice is really the voice of Jo's thoughts, like a voice in a dream. Try to make this voice sound strange – perhaps by speaking down a hollow tube (but make sure it does not sound funny).

### Just don't call us names
1 The brothers and sisters in this poem should sound sarcastic and annoyed. They should

surround James who is unable to escape their complaints.

2 Your teacher may wish to use this poem in a drama lesson, the class acting out the lines as you recite them – chaotic, perhaps, but fun.

## Our street

In between each verse of this poem you could do some actions. For example, for Verse 1 you could all wave and say hello to an imaginary passer-by. For Verse 2 you could look serious, mime the closing of curtains and then turn your back on the audience. For Verse 3 you could look as though you are inviting people in. For Verse 4 you could shout threateningly at passers-by. For Verse 5 the first four speakers could gather round the fifth as if she were Granny, and then begin a tea party.

## My tree

1 All the group should say the first four words of each verse, the part in italics.

2 Each verse could be mimed, first by the performers, then by the audience.

## Sometimes my sister

1 One voice in this poem is what the girl says aloud to herself. The other voice (in *italics*) is what she thinks. So it would make sense if the two performers faced each other, one being the mirror image of the other. An empty picture frame or card frame between the two would give the idea of a mirror.

2 The first speaker should mime the actions to go with her words; the second speaker should mirror these. The first speaker should pause in her actions when the second speaker says her words. Great stress should be laid upon the word "Perhaps" in the last line; the girl is still not quite sure about it.

## Unhappy boy

1 Mime would go well with this poem. The members of the chorus should surround the boy, facing him as they say their words the first time. In the second verse the boy runs around the ring of the chorus and threatens each one of them. They each turn their back on him, facing outwards. As the boy juggles with a stone during the third verse, the chorus edges away from him. By the end of the poem the space around him is so big he is on his own.

## A playground chant

1 Chant this as you would any playground chant. Stand in a row, with Speaker 2 in the middle. Speaker 2 turns and pats hands rhythmically with Speaker 1 as the first verse is being said. Speaker 2 then says the second verse to the audience while the other two pat hands. Speaker 2 then turns and pats hands with Speaker 3 as the third verse is said.

2 For a second performance, invite the audience to join in the choruses.

## Sporting wishes

1 Once you have decided who is playing which part, practise the parts that you all say together. Once you can say them clearly, work out the mime actions you could all do to go with each verse. For example, you could do swimming strokes, knock a cricket ball for six, run on the spot, and so on. Try to make sure that everyone moves in the same way at the same time.

2 Before you say your own part, do a short mime about your sport and continue it after you have finished, while the parts for you all are being said.

3 Throughout the poem, Speaker 6 – the tiddlywinker – could be set a little apart, perhaps

shaking his or her head after each verse. This will lead the audience to expect something a little different at the end.

### The pink party
1 Shout the word "PINK" in Verse 2.
2 A few of the verses can be said with the appropriate actions: wiping feet, blowing up a balloon, eating.
3 The chorus need not necessarily be said by many voices at once. You can, if you wish, share out the lines. Try both ways to find the one that sounds best.

### The midnight party
1 The speaker playing the part of the owl should stand in the centre surrounded by the other animals.
2 As a performance, the poem would be better if each speaker wore an animal mask. The witch needs to look as scary as possible.
3 The Narrator needs a big book from which to read his or her part.
4 When everyone speaks together, match actions to the words.

### Mourning the moon
1 Try performing this with stick puppets.
2 A sickle moon is very important to this poem. Either hold or pin one up where everyone can see it.

### Down by the stream
1 The first speaker is the one who tells the story. He or she should take centre stage. The rest add the details.
2 Practise the chorus carefully. Do you want actions to go with the words? If so, what would look best?

## Winter's song

1 Try painting the following to go with your performance: wild birds in the sky; a sunset at sea; leaves falling; animals hibernating; a robin in the snow.

2 For a repeat performance of the poem, ask the audience to join in the chorus. You or your teacher will need to write up the words so that everyone can read them.

## A winter chant

1 The three people who say this chant could be on a walk through the snow. Try saying the verses as you trudge in a circle, crunching your feet (Verse 1), and flapping your hands (Verse 2). On each line which begins with the word "here", point to the ground as if you have just noticed something on the walk.

2 You could write up the words of the chorus for the audience to read during a second performance.

3 The third verse is different from the first two. Is there any way you could make it sound more mysterious?

## Never, always

1 Face each other and chant this poem rapidly, barely pausing for breath until you get to the line "Never see it inside out". It should sound like an argument – but not a bad-tempered one. The poem begins to slow down at the end, from the words "Never pinch it".

2 Once you have performed the poem, you could ask the whole class to join in. One half of the class echoes the first voice, the other half echoes the second.

## Night street

1 Try making a recording of soft, heavy footsteps.

This can be played as a background to the poem.

2  Sit on a desk or table with your heads to one side on your hands, to suggest sleep. Stay asleep except when it is your turn to speak. After the last chorus you should all be wide awake.

3  Your actions should show your fear, but don't overdo them or you will make your audience laugh and ruin the effect you are trying to create.

4  You could repeat the poem, inviting your audience to join in the chorus. Practise it with them first.

### Into the sea
1  If possible, ask your teacher to play a recording of the sea beating its waves on the beach. If you can use the recording during your performance, it will create the right atmosphere for the poem.

2  There should be two performers for this poem, although only one of them speaks. Think about why the second person says nothing. Does he or she give the speaker their hand, or hold it back?

3  The chorus should sound slow, mysterious and a little threatening.

### The Pied Piper's return
1  The mood of this poem changes from liveliness to fear, and ends on a note of mystery. The first two verses and chorus will sound full of fun. Then in the next two verses doubt creeps in and the speed slows down. After the piper speaks – or sings – there is a feeling of alarm as the children feel trapped in the dance.

2  This poem is best performed with a line of you in pairs in a large space such as the school hall.

3  If possible, the piper should softly play a recorder when he or she is not speaking. Alternatively, you could have flute music in the background with the piper pretending to play.

**4** Before you perform the poem, remind your audience of the original Pied Piper poem by Robert Browning.

### The spirit of place
**1** There are three parts to this poem. The first part (down to "the old tree trembled") is slow. The second part (down to "it shrieked for escape") is loud, quick and dramatic. The last part slows down but then builds to a climax in the last two lines. Allow a good pause between the three parts.
**2** You could display four paintings to go with your poem: an island with an old tree in a valley; a large egg containing a fierce, prehistoric creature; the tree shattered in a hurricane with the creature breaking out of the egg; the creature on the shore about to plunge into the sea.

### The nursery ward
**1** This poem is really a mini-play. You have a choice: you can either act it, using some extra people to play the Duke of York's men; or, more easily, you can record it as a radio play. Talk about this choice with your teacher.
**2** Whichever approach you choose, your performance will be improved by some sound effects: a telephone ringing, patients groaning and sneezing, a "terrible cry" and so on.
**3** The Narrator should stand apart, as if reading the story from a book.
**4** The parts where everyone joins in will need to be practised carefully so that the words are clear. Try limiting these parts to a separate group of three or four people.